SCIENCE ON
SHACKLETON'S
EXPEDITION

by Tammy Enz

CAPSTONE PRESS
a capstone imprint

Capstone Captivate is published by Capstone Press, an imprint of Capstone.
1710 Roe Crest Drive
North Mankato, Minnesota 56003
www.capstonepub.com

Library of Congress Cataloging-in-Publication Data
Names: Enz, Tammy, author.
Title: Science on Shackleton's expedition / by Tammy Enz.
Description: North Mankato, Minnesota : Capstone Captivate is published by Capstone Press, [2021] | Series: The Science of History | Includes bibliographical references and index. | Audience: Ages 8-11 years | Audience: Grades 4-6 | Summary: "Sir Ernest Henry Shackleton led an expedition across Antarctica in 1914. Did you know that science played a big role in this dangerous journey? Learn how weather patterns affected the explorer in Antarctica. Find out the science behind Shackleton's ship, The Endurance . And discover how modern technology is being used to find out even more about this adventure more than 100 years later"-- Provided by publisher. Identifiers: LCCN 2021002860 (print) | LCCN 2021002861 (ebook) | ISBN 9781496695741 (Library Binding) | ISBN 9781496696922 (Paperback) | ISBN 9781977159151 (PDF) | ISBN 9781977159236 (Kindle Edition) Subjects: LCSH: Antarctica--Discovery and exploration--British--Juvenile literature. | Scientific expeditions--Antarctica--History--20th century. | Shackleton, Ernest Henry, Sir, 1874-1922--Juvenile literature. |Imperial Trans-Antarctic Expedition (1914-1917)--Juvenile literature. | Endurance (Ship)--Juvenile literature. Classification: LCC G872.B8 E69 2021 (print) | LCC G872.B8 (ebook) | DDC 919.8904--dc23 LC record available at https://lccn.loc.gov/2021002860 LC ebook record available at https://lccn.loc.gov/2021002861

Editorial Credits
Editors, Angie Kaelberer and Aaron Sautter; Designer, Kazuko Collins; Media Researcher, Svetlana Zhurkin; Production Specialist, Kathy McColley

Image Credits
Alamy: Smith Archive, 36; Capstone: 27; Getty Images: Hulton Archive, 4 (bottom), Royal Geographical Society/Frank Hurley, 29 (top), 38, 45 (top), Royal Geographical Society/Herbert Ponting, 25, University of Cambridge/Scott Polar Research Institute/Frank Hurley, cover (bottom), 10, 16, 22, 23, 45 (bottom); iStockphoto: Echinophoria, 13; Library of Congress: 4 (top), Frank Hurley, 12, 17, 19, 21, 31, 32; Newscom: World History Archive, 14; North Wind Picture Archives: 8; Shutterstock: Alexey Koldunov, 29 (bottom), ArtMediaWorx, 34, Designua, 7 (bottom), Douglas Olivares, 39, Ian D M Robertson, 26, Janelle Lugge, 41, KamimiArt (design element), 1 (bottom and throughout), Peter Hermes Furian, 5, 9, 43 (bottom), polar man john, 7 (top), Prostock-studio, 35, Rainer Lesniewski, 15, Scorpp, cover (top), 1 (top), Thomas Barrat, 43 (top), Triff, 33

TABLE OF CONTENTS

Words in **bold** text are included in the glossary.

CHAPTER 1

ANTARCTICA OR BUST!

Ernest Shackleton was a man with a dream. He wanted to be the first explorer to reach the South Pole. In 1908 he nearly succeeded. He came close but had to turn back due to weather conditions and low supplies. Another explorer, Roald Amundsen of Norway, beat him to the pole. Amundsen placed a flag on the South Pole in 1911.

Ernest Shackleton

Ernest Shackleton led the British Antarctic Expedition from 1907 to 1909. He came within 112 miles (180 kilometers) of the South Pole before being forced to turn back.

But Shackleton wasn't ready to give up. His new goal was to be the first to travel across Antarctica through the South Pole. He selected 27 men and 69 mixed-breed sled dogs to join the Imperial Trans-Antarctic Expedition.

Everyone knew Shackleton's team faced incredible odds. Antarctica is the most remote of Earth's seven continents. It's bitterly cold and lies under a layer of ice about 9,000 feet (2,700 meters) thick.

Shackleton was prepared for a dangerous adventure. But he had no idea how much his crew would have to face.

Fact

The warmest temperature ever recorded at the South Pole was 9.9 degrees Fahrenheit (-12.3 degrees Celsius).

Shackleton's Planned Route

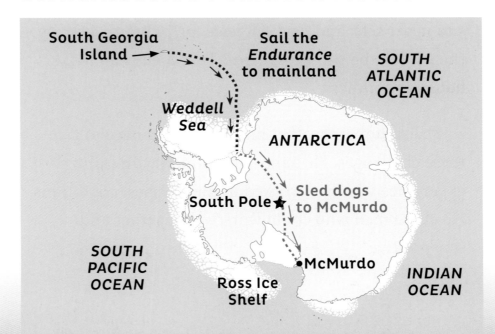

South Georgia Island →

Sail the *Endurance* to mainland

SOUTH ATLANTIC OCEAN

Weddell Sea

ANTARCTICA

Sled dogs to McMurdo

South Pole ★

SOUTH PACIFIC OCEAN

McMurdo

Ross Ice Shelf

INDIAN OCEAN

A LAND OF EXTREMES

Shackleton planned to use every bit of science and technology available at the time. He packed the best navigational tools and equipment. Today explorers use satellite technology to find their way and communicate. But Shackleton had only a few handheld tools and experienced explorers to help him.

Shackleton knew the dangers of exploring Antarctica. This continent not only has extreme weather conditions. It also has extremes of sunlight and darkness. Earth spins on an axis that tilts. That means for half the year, Antarctica faces toward the sun. For the other half of the year, it faces away from the sun. The sun is always above the horizon in summer. The sun never sets, and daylight lasts for 24 hours. During the winter, the sun never rises. That means up to 24 hours of darkness.

Shackleton knew that his crew would have to face these challenges. He hand-picked men with sailing experience who had worked in the harshest conditions. He chose men who could work well together and stay positive.

Antarctica receives very little sunshine during the winter months.

Earth's Axis

Earth's tilted axis also causes changes in the seasons. Antarctica is located in the Southern Hemisphere. Its seasons are the opposite of those in the Northern Hemisphere. Summer in the Southern Hemisphere starts on December 21 and winter begins on June 21.

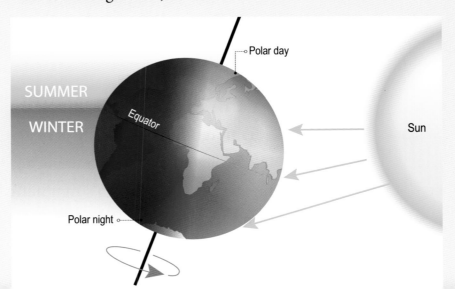

SUMMER

WINTER

Equator

Polar day

Polar night

Sun

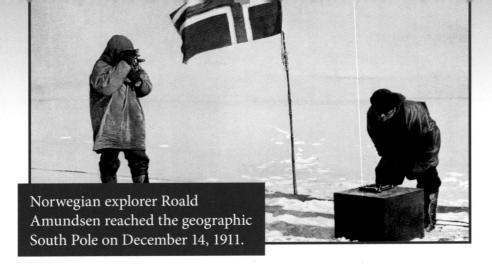

Norwegian explorer Roald Amundsen reached the geographic South Pole on December 14, 1911.

Shackleton would know he reached the South Pole when he saw Amundsen's flag. But how did Amundsen know that he had found the actual South Pole?

There are actually two South Poles—the geographic South Pole and the magnetic South Pole. Imagine Earth as a ball with a stick running through its center. When the ball spins around the stick, the geographic poles are located at the ends of the stick.

But Earth's magnetic poles are different than the geographic poles. Earth's core is made from molten iron. It acts like a giant magnet. Magnets also have north and south poles. Earth's magnetic north pole is near the South Pole. Its magnetic south pole is near the North Pole. Magnetic poles can be found using a compass. A compass needle points to Earth's magnetic poles. People can use compasses to help find their way.

Amundsen placed his flag at the geographic South Pole. He used a **theodolite** to locate it. This tool measures the sun's angle from the horizon. The sun's path through the sky can be measured based on the time of year. Amundsen measured the sun's angle for several days until he discovered the exact location of the South Pole.

Earth's Poles

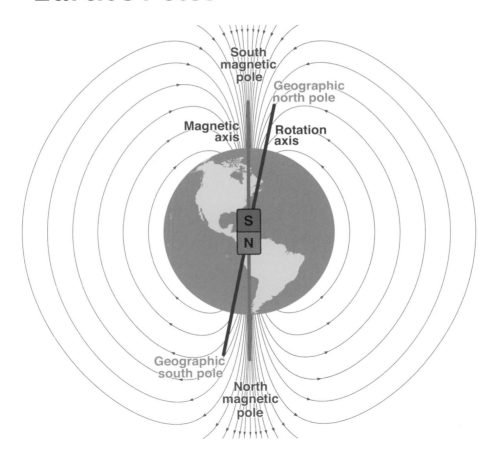

A STURDY SHIP

Shackleton's ship, the *Endurance*, left South Georgia Island on December 5, 1914. This mostly empty island is near the southern tip of South America. The water near Antarctica was very icy that summer. The ship needed to cross the Weddell Sea before winter.

As the *Endurance* sailed toward Antarctica, the sturdy ship broke through thick ice floes in the Weddell Sea.

But the *Endurance* was up to the task. It had a 50-horsepower steam engine that could burn both coal and oil. The *Endurance* could travel at a maximum speed of 10.2 knots. A knot is about 1.15 miles (1.85 km) per hour.

Steam ships had been around since the early 1800s. Steam engines burn fuel for heat. The heat boils water that turns to steam. Steam builds up pressure that moves a **piston** up and down. The piston turns a propeller to power the ship.

The *Endurance* rammed through floating sheets of ice called ice floes to make its way south. After about six weeks, the ship was within 100 miles (160 km) of Antarctica. It only had one day of sailing left before it reached land. But as the water became colder, thicker ice formed. The ice floes closed in until the ship was frozen in the ice. It was January 18, 1915.

CHAPTER 2

PACKED IN ICE

Shackleton's crew worked for days to break the *Endurance* free from the ice. But the ship wouldn't budge. The crew loaded their lifeboats on **sledges** and tried to cross the ice. But ice ridges prevented them from going very far. The men were stuck until spring thaw.

The *Endurance* became trapped in thick pack ice in January 1915.

Ice ridges formed by pressure from wind and ocean currents can rise 40 feet (12 m) high or more.

Icebergs are created when chunks of ice break off from glaciers or ice shelves. The part of the iceberg floating below the water is six to seven times larger than the part above water.

Ice ridges form differently than icebergs do. Wind and ocean movements push ice sheets against each other. The sheets buckle or one sheet slides beneath the other and pushes it up to form a ridge.

Temperature changes also cause expanding and contracting ice to form ridges. When water freezes, it expands by 9 percent. The swelling ice forms ridges.

GRAVITY FORCES AT WORK

Tides and currents are always at work in the oceans. The sun and moon are far from Earth. But they still pull on Earth and its oceans with gravity. These forces cause waves called tides that crash into land and ice masses. Tides move water up and down.

No Communications

In the early 1900s ships could use radios to send signals. These communications are sent on invisible electromagnetic waves. Radio communications need a transmitter device to send a signal and a receiver to receive the signal. The two must be in range of one another. Unfortunately, the *Endurance* was too far from any receivers to send a signal for help.

Currents also move water. Currents are like rivers running through the ocean. Temperature changes cause currents. Near the equator, the sun warms the ocean water. This warm water flows toward the cold water near the poles. The cold water moves toward the equator, where it warms. The cycle repeats, causing constant currents.

Through the first nine months of 1915, tides and currents helped push ice and the frozen *Endurance* 1,300 miles (2,092 km) north. The ship's crew could only watch the tides and currents carry them back north and farther away from Antarctica.

Ocean Currents near Antarctica

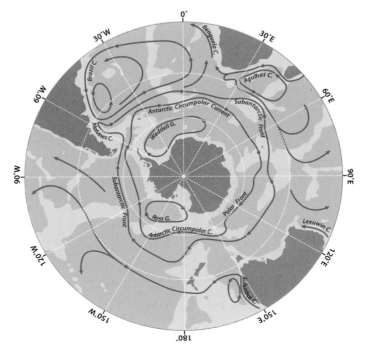

STAYING HEALTHY

Shackleton knew that he needed to keep his men healthy and positive while they waited. He made the men get off the ship and exercise themselves and the sled dogs.

Shackleton wanted to avoid muscle **atrophy**. When a body doesn't move much, the muscles shrink. It becomes difficult to move. The men needed their strength to survive what was ahead of them.

Shackleton's crew played games like soccer on the ice to get exercise and to lift their spirits.

Shackleton brought 69 sled dogs on the expedition. His crew made sure the dogs were well fed while they were stuck on the ice.

The men also kept the dogs in top shape. If they made it to Antarctica, they would need the dogs to pull their sleds. Sled dogs are bred to perform in the hardest conditions. Their thick fur helps keep them warm. Their bodies can also draw energy from fats in their blood rather than from their muscles. The cells of sled dogs have very dense mitochondria, which is the part of a cell that produces energy. Hundreds of years of breeding have helped the dogs develop this ability. It helps prevent their muscles from wearing out during long races.

Fact

A sled dog needs to eat about 12,000 calories per day when racing. Humans need about 2,000 calories per day.

CHAPTER 3

OCEAN CAMP

Late October was springtime in Antarctica. Finally the ice began to melt and shift. But this was bad news for the *Endurance*. The shifting ice began to crush the ship. Eventually it tipped and began to take on water. The men frantically tried to pump out the water.

The ship was heavy. It weighed 348 tons. But it was **buoyant**. Buoyant objects are less dense than water, so they float. Most of the inside of a ship is filled with air, which is much less dense than water. This low density allows the ship to float. When a ship fills with water, it's no longer less dense than the water around it. It begins to sink.

The men finally gave up hope. They packed what they could, including food and medicine, in their three lifeboats. Then they and their dogs left the ship. They watched as the *Endurance* sank beneath the ice. The men and dogs were left floating on an ice floe.

After drifting for months, the *Endurance* was finally crushed by the powerful sea ice. The ship sank on November 21, 1915.

CAMPING ON THE ICE

The men tried to pull the loaded lifeboats across the ice. But icy ridges prevented them from traveling far. They set up camp on the ice floe and called it "Ocean Camp." Some quick thinking helped make life on the floe bearable. The men used what they knew of science to survive on the ice. The crew members had saved parts of the ship. They used parts of the ship's boiler to make small stoves. But stoves without fuel would be useless. So the men used fatty penguin skin and seal blubber for fuel.

Nature provides some mammals in cold areas, such as seals and whales, with a unique feature called blubber. This thick layer of fat is between an animal's muscles and skin. Half these animals' weight can consist of blubber. The blubber keeps the animals warm. It's also buoyant, so it helps animals stay afloat in cold Antarctic waters.

Fact
The three loaded lifeboats weighed 1 ton each.

People can eat blubber for food. Humans also use it as a fuel source. Cooking blubber over a fire creates an oil. It can be used like any other heating oil.

After the ship sank, Shackleton and his men set up camp with a few tents. Simple stoves provided warmth and a way to cook food and process animal blubber.

STAYING WARM

To stay warm Shackleton's men huddled in their sleeping bags made of reindeer fur. They also wore wool clothing to keep out the cold. Wool is the perfect material for cold, wet weather. Its fibers absorb and trap water. It can absorb 30 percent of its weight in water without feeling wet. The water chemically binds to the insides of the wool fiber. The process of chemical bonding creates heat. For this reason, a person can actually feel warm in wet wool clothing.

Glacier Goggles

The adventurers wore sun goggles to protect their eyes from the sun's blinding reflection off the ice. The sun's ultraviolet (UV) rays can cause eye damage. Sun goggles block UV rays like sunglasses. They also wrap around to prevent UV rays from seeping under or around the glasses.

Wool clothing and tightly woven gabardine jackets helped keep the men warm in the cold climate.

The men also had gabardine jackets. These jackets were a must-have for explorers in the early 1900s. Gabardine fabric is made from very tightly woven wool or cotton. The jackets were lightweight, breathable, and waterproof.

The men struggled through the spring months on the ice floe. Supplies ran low. Hunger, thirst, and exposure were constant threats. Overcome with hunger, the men made a desperate decision. They decided to kill and eat their dogs to stay alive.

CHAPTER 4

OFF TO ELEPHANT ISLAND

SAFE STOPS

The crew's ice floe was about 5 feet (1.5 m) thick at first. But it was melting and shrinking fast. The crew members pulled out their sounding machine to find the water depth.

The *Endurance*'s sounding machine had a long wire wound around a reel. The wire was marked at each fathom. One fathom is 6 feet (1.83 m) long. A weight was attached to the end of the wire. The weight was dropped in the water. When it sank to the ocean floor, the crew read the depth in fathoms off the wire. Beneath the crew's ice floe was 2,000 fathoms of icy cold water.

Sounding machines were used to measure ocean depths. The readings helped sailors know if the water was deep enough for their ship's hull.

One night as the men slept, a loud crack filled the air. The melting ice floe had split in half! The ice was melting. The men needed to find land fast. Elephant Island was their best bet, but it was 100 miles (161 km) away and deserted. However, it was their only hope.

Fact

The word *fathom* comes from an Old English word meaning "outstretched arms." It describes the distance between a man's fingertips with his arms outstretched.

A RISKY JOURNEY

The men set out in their three small lifeboats. They fought snow **squalls** and killer whales. Violent winds pushed them one way. A strong current pulled them the other way.

The men dropped canvas sea anchors to help them stay on course. When these large canvas bags filled with water, they provided **drag**. The drag helped keep winds from blowing the boats too far off course.

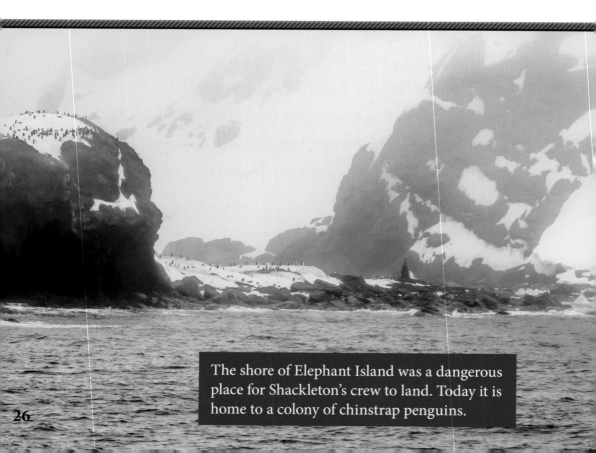

The shore of Elephant Island was a dangerous place for Shackleton's crew to land. Today it is home to a colony of chinstrap penguins.

Riptide Formation

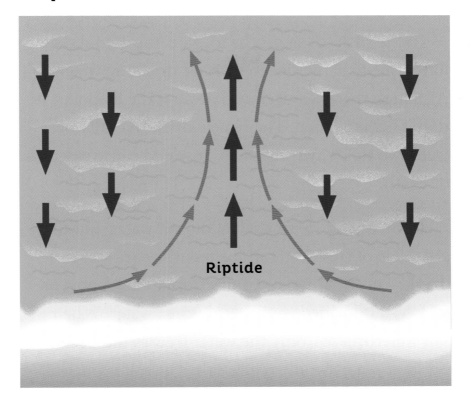

Riptide

As the boats neared the shore of Elephant Island, dangerous riptides swirled. Riptides occur along shorelines. In areas with offshore sandbars and reefs, tidewaters crash into them. The water then can't flow easily back to the ocean. The water rushes along the shore instead. When it finds a break in the reef, the water rushes through it like in a draining sink. Boats caught in riptides can be swamped and crushed.

BACK ON DRY LAND

In the rush to get off the ice floe, the men didn't have time to gather ice to melt for drinking water. Although there was water all around the lifeboats, it didn't help the men. They knew drinking salty ocean water would **dehydrate** them. It would cause sickness or death.

Icebergs and ice floes float on salt water. But they are made of freshwater. If melted, they are safe to drink. This floating ice comes from glacier snow or ice crystals formed from freezing sea water. When salt water freezes, only the water freezes into ice crystals. Ice naturally repels salt. The salt is pushed to the surface of the ice, leaving frozen freshwater in the ice floes.

The men paddled for seven days on choppy waters to get to Elephant Island. It was the first time they had been on solid land in 497 days. The thirsty men were grateful to find freshwater in an island stream.

Shackleton's crew finally stood on solid ground after landing on Elephant Island on April 15, 1916.

Seasickness

Besides thirst, the men suffered from seasickness. This condition is caused by an imbalance in the inner ear. The fluid in the ear bounces around with the boat's movement. But a person's eyes see the steady area inside the boat. The body tries to respond to the two different sensations. It sends out hormones that can make people feel dizzy and throw up. At the time of Shackleton's expedition, the only cure for seasickness was to try to get used to it.

CHAPTER 5

BACK TO SOUTH GEORGIA

The men huddled on Elephant Island as they waited out a blizzard. After the storm, Shackleton decided to take five men and head back to South Georgia—the island where they had begun their trip. It was more than 800 miles (1,300 km) away.

Instead of trying to cross Antarctica, Shackleton had a new mission. He had to focus on getting his men home safely. The ship's carpenter, Harry McNeish, prepared the small *James Caird* lifeboat for the trip. He waterproofed the boat with a mixture of flour, oil paint, and seal blood. He attached canvas to the deck to keep out water from storms and waves.

After landing on Elephant Island, Shackleton's crew set up camp in a safe area they called Point Wild.

The carpenter packed the lifeboat with about 1 ton of rock **ballast**. Boats without much cargo float high on the water. They are easily tossed about by ocean waves. Boats need ballast to weigh them down so they sit lower in the water. This makes it harder for wind and waves to topple the boat. The men also melted ice for fresh drinking water and stored it in kegs for the trip.

BACK TO SEA

Nine days after landing on Elephant Island, Shackleton was out to sea again. He and five crew members—Frank Worsley, Harry McNeish, Thomas Crean, Timothy McCarthy, and John Vincent—headed north to catch the westerlies. These strong winds blow from west to east. They are caused by warm air from the equator blowing toward the poles. Warm air moves toward the colder parts of Earth to try to equalize the temperature.

Shackleton and five crewmen launched the *James Caird* from Elephant Island on April 24, 1916. Shackleton was determined to reach South Georgia Island to find help for the rest of his crew.

Ship navigators used sextants to help determine their location on a map.

The men soon sailed north out of the ice zone. Worsley, the ship's navigator, waited for a break in the clouds. As the waves tossed the boat, Worsley measured the sun's position with his sextant. This instrument uses mirrors to help measure the sun's angle from the horizon. Sailors need to know the sun's position and the time of the measurement. With this information, they can use a **nautical almanac** to find their position.

FIGHTING THIRST

The men bounced along, soaked by pounding waves. Their one luxury was two hot meals a day cooked on a Primus stove. They held the stove between their feet so it wouldn't fall overboard.

The Primus stove used pressurized kerosene to create a very hot flame. The kerosene was pressurized with a hand pump that pushed the fuel from a tank through a series of pipes. The pressure allowed for complete combustion, which is the chemical reaction between oxygen and fuel. Complete combustion means all the fuel burns. None is left to create soot. It is a very efficient use of fuel. The crew didn't have a large supply of kerosene, so they saved it for cooking meals.

Primus Stove

top ring

burner

spirit cup

rising tube

pump

tank

Vital Water

People need large quantities of water every day to survive. Water makes up about 60 percent of our bodies. We depend on water to form cells, regulate body temperature, and flush out waste. Adult men need about 13 cups (3 liters) of water each day.

Storms like the men had never seen before pounded the little boat. At times, waves covered the canvas deck and created a layer of ice several inches thick.

Even worse, their biggest enemy—thirst—was back. After thirteen days, they discovered their last keg of water was salty and undrinkable. They could drink only 8 ounces (237 milliliters) of water per day.

After two weeks, the men saw kelp plants and large birds called shags. These were signs of land nearby. Birds stay close to land, and kelp grows near shores.

BATTLING FOR LIFE

The men had made it to South Georgia Island. They were anxious to get to shore. But there was no safe place to land. On the fourteenth day, they faced the most furious storm yet. The men frantically tried to keep the boat away from shore. They couldn't risk crashing into the cliffs.

Before landing at South Georgia Island, Shackleton and his men had to battle through one of the worst storms they'd ever seen.

For two days the men battled the massive gale. These storms have winds of 34 to 47 knots (39 to 54 miles; 63 to 87 km) per hour. To keep the *James Caird* afloat, crew members used a canvas bag as an anchor. The drag from the anchor kept the boat facing into the wind. This kept some ocean waves from crashing into and flooding the boat. Still, the crew had to keep bailing and pumping water out of the boat. The freezing water and cold wind also created a heavy coat of ice on the small boat. The men had to chip away the ice and throw spare gear overboard to reduce the boat's weight.

Finally, after a 16-day trip, the crew made landfall on May 10, 1916. They had survived one of the most dangerous boat trips in history. But they were on the south side of the island. This wasn't good. They needed to be on the north side, where the Norwegian whaling village was.

Fact

Shackleton and his crew later learned that a 500-ton steamer ship nearby was lost in the same storm they had survived.

Back on Elephant Island, the rest of the crew created a shelter with the remaining lifeboats and waited for Shackleton's return.

Meanwhile, all wasn't well back on Elephant Island. The remaining 22 explorers turned over the two remaining lifeboats to use as shelter. Besides boredom and hunger, the men suffered from health problems. One had a heart attack, but he recovered. Another suffered from an infected tooth, which had to be pulled.

The worst case was a young explorer with frostbite on his toes. The frostbite turned to gangrene. Gangrene occurs when body tissue dies near a wound. It can cause infections that lead to death. The only cure is to cut away the dead tissue. The explorer's toes needed to be removed to save his life.

Fortunately, the ship's crew included two doctors, Alexander Macklin and James McIlroy. These doctors used an early form of **anesthesia** called chloroform during surgeries. Chloroform is a chemical that people breathe in. It slows down their nervous system and reduces the pain messages sent to the brain.

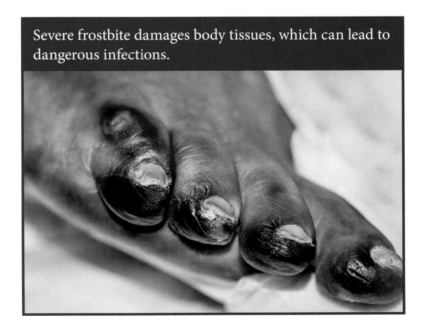
Severe frostbite damages body tissues, which can lead to dangerous infections.

CHAPTER 6

THE IMPOSSIBLE HIKE

With only eight days of rest, Shackleton headed out again. This time he took two of the healthiest men, Worsley and Crean, with him. They planned to hike across South Georgia Island to the whaling village on the north side. The distance was about 20 miles (32 km) over dangerous, mountainous land.

No one had explored the island's inner area before. The men didn't know what to expect. All they could see were mountains and glaciers. They knew they wouldn't be able to stop to sleep, so they didn't pack sleeping bags. They brought only a Primus stove, food, a rope, an ax, and some navigational tools.

Shackleton and two of his men decided to hike across the rugged terrain of the island to find rescue. The other men stayed at King Haakon Bay where the *James Caird* had landed.

The men used a compass to determine their direction. They also used a chronometer. This timepiece can keep time even when bumped around. Chronometers were used before watches were invented. Early explorers needed to know the time so they could find their location using a navigational almanac and the position of the sun.

JOURNEY TO SAFETY

Icy glaciers with hidden crevices made hiking across the island dangerous. The ship's carpenter created crampons for hiking. He removed screws from the lifeboat and drove them into the soles of the men's boots. This created **friction** to help them walk on the ice.

The men left at 3 a.m. on May 19 during a full moon. They trudged about 5,000 feet (1,500 m) up rocky slopes. But they couldn't find a way down the other side. As darkness set in, the men feared they would freeze to death. They came up with a last-ditch plan. They coiled the rope into a makeshift sled. All three hopped aboard and slid down the slope. They quickly plunged more than 1,000 feet (300 m).

The men were shocked to have made it down the slope alive. But there was no time to celebrate. They still had a long way to go. After hours of hiking, they stumbled into the whaling station at 3 p.m. on May 20. Their trip had taken 36 hours.

After a grueling 36-hour trek, Shackleton and the others finally arrived at the whaling station on the north side of the island.

Shackleton's Route and Timeline

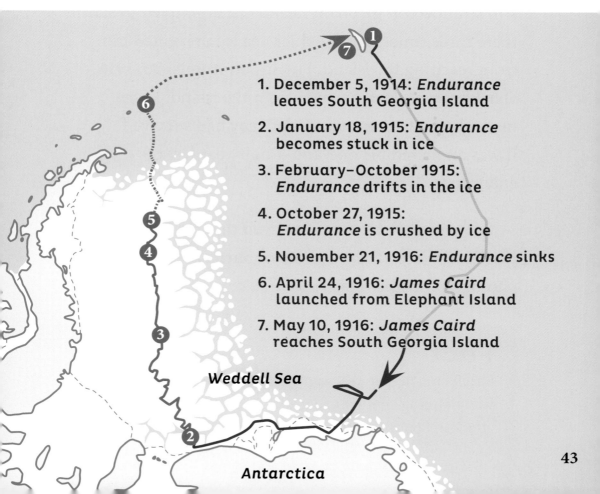

1. December 5, 1914: *Endurance* leaves South Georgia Island

2. January 18, 1915: *Endurance* becomes stuck in ice

3. February–October 1915: *Endurance* drifts in the ice

4. October 27, 1915: *Endurance* is crushed by ice

5. November 21, 1916: *Endurance* sinks

6. April 24, 1916: *James Caird* launched from Elephant Island

7. May 10, 1916: *James Caird* reaches South Georgia Island

Weddell Sea

Antarctica

RESCUED!

One of the world's most incredible journeys was over. But Shackleton's work wasn't done. He still had to collect the three men on the other side of South Georgia Island. He sent the whaling ship *Samson* to the other side of the island to pick up McNeish, McCarthy, and Vincent.

Shackleton also still needed to rescue the 22 men still stranded on Elephant Island. He attempted to sail there three times, but the thick sea ice prevented him from reaching the island. Finally, on August 30, 1916, Shackleton rescued his men from the island. Every man who had set out on the journey had survived. It was an incredible one-and-a-half-year test of endurance.

Some important items survived the trip. Frank Hurley, the expedition's photographer, saved his photographic glass plates.

Fact

Shackleton desperately wanted to return to Antarctica. He was planning another trip in 1922 when he died of a heart attack in South Georgia. He was buried on the island.

More than four months after leaving Elephant Island, Shackleton was finally able to rescue the rest of his crew that had been left behind.

Early photography used glass plates to create images. The plates were covered with light-sensitive **silver halide** crystals. When exposed to light, the crystals change chemically. The more light they are exposed to, the more they change. The changes are invisible until the chemicals are set. Then they are developed into an image.

Frank Hurley

Thanks to Hurley and the science of photography, glimpses of Shackleton's amazing journey are available for us to see today. His images tell the story of the historic expedition and courage of the men who tried to cross the bottom of the world.

GLOSSARY

anesthesia (a-nuhs-THEE-zhuh)—a gas or injection that prevents pain during treatments and surgeries

ballast (BA-luhst)—any heavy material that adds weight to an object

buoyant (BOY-uhnt)—able to float

dehydrate (dee-HY-drayt)—to dry out

drag (DRAG)—the force that slows down the motion of an object moving through air or water

friction (FRIK-shuhn)—a force created when two objects rub together; friction slows down movement

nautical almanac (NAW-tuh-kuhl AWL-muh-nak)—a book with positions of sun and stars used for navigation

piston (PIS-tuhn)—the part of an engine that moves up and down within a tube and transfers force

silver halide (SIL-vuhr HAH-lyde)—a chemical used in photography

sledge (SLEJ)—a large, heavy snow sled

squall (SKWOL)—a sudden strong wind, often accompanied by rain or snow

theodolite (THEE-uh-duh-lyte)—a tool for measuring angles of objects from the horizon

READ MORE

Doeden, Matt. *Surviving Antarctica: Ernest Shackleton.* Minneapolis: Lerner Publications, 2019.

Loh-Hagan, Virginia. *Ernest Shackleton: Survival in the Antarctic.* Ann Arbor, MI: Cherry Lake Publishing, 2018.

Olson, Tod. *Lost in the Antarctic: The Doomed Voyage of the Endurance.* New York: Scholastic, 2019.

INTERNET SITES

Antarctica Facts
www.kids-world-travel-guide.com/antarctica-facts.html

Ernest Shackleton
academickids.com/encyclopedia/index.php/Ernest_Shackleton

Ernest Shackleton Facts for Kids
kids.kiddle.co/Ernest_Shackleton

INDEX